The Cricket in Times Square

by
George Selden

Student Packet

Written by
Jean Jamieson

Contains masters for:

1	Prereading Activity
10	Vocabulary Activities
1	Study Guide (three pages)
2	Critical Thinking Activities
4	Writing Activities
1	Mathematics Activity
2	Comprehension Activities
1	Comprehension Quiz (two levels)
1	Unit Exam (two levels) Four Sections
PLUS	Detailed Answer Key

Note

The text used to prepare this guide was the Dell Yearling softcover edition. The page references may differ in the hardcover or other paperback editions.

Please note: Please assess the appropriateness of this book for the age level and maturity of your students prior to reading and discussing it with your class.

ISBN 1-56137-835-6

Printed in the United States of America.

To order, contact your local school supply store, or—

Novel Units, Inc.
P.O. Box 97
Bulverde, TX 78163-0097

Web site: www.educyberstor.com

Name______________________________

Crickets

Directions: Read the following for information. Answer the questions at the bottom of the page.

Crickets are slender, chirping, jumping insects. They are closely related to grasshoppers and cockroaches. True crickets are usually green or brown, with long antennae.

Crickets have hind legs that are designed for jumping. Their hearing organs are located on their front legs.

Most crickets have wings. The males, and some females, "chirp" or "sing" by rapidly drawing a file-like structure on one forewing over a thickened vein on the opposing wing. Cricket-sounds are usually made at night. However, some crickets sing by day from dense vegetation.

The cricket-sounds attract mates. Chirping males may defend their territories, sometimes by physical combat. Most crickets live through a single annual generation.

Young crickets, called nymphs, resemble the adults. They reach full size after six to twelve molts. The nymphs eat leaves or roots.

There are different kinds of crickets. They do not look alike. Field crickets are the best known. They are often seen outdoors under boards and other debris. House crickets enter houses in Europe and parts of the United States. They are known for their cheery chirping. Tree crickets are pale green. Mole crickets have enlarged forelegs.

Mark each statement with a "T" for True or an "F" for False.

______ 1. Crickets are related to grasshoppers and cockroaches.

______ 2. Crickets cannot jump.

______ 3. Crickets make sounds with their wings.

______ 4. Young crickets are called nymphs.

______ 5. All crickets look alike.

Name______________________________

Study Questions

Write a brief answer to each study question as you read the book at home or in class. Use the questions for review before group discussions and before your final test.

Chapters One—Five (Pages 1-41)

1. What is Tucker?
2. Where does Tucker live?
3. How does Tucker provide himself with food?
4. Who is Mario, and what does he do at the Times Square subway station?
5. What causes the unusual sound heard by Mario and Tucker?
6. What does Mario do with the cricket?
7. What do Mama and Papa Bellini think of the cricket?
8. What decision is made regarding the cricket as a pet for Mario?
9. What are Tucker's favorite activities?
10. What food is the cause of Chester's move from Connecticut?
11. How does Chester get from Connecticut to New York?
12. What is unusual about the relationship between Tucker and Harry Cat?
13. What do Harry and Tucker predict for the future of the Bellini newsstand? Why?
14. What is a long-hair?
15. What does Chester see above New York, and above the whole world, that is familiar to him?
16. What is Chester's usual food back in the meadow?
17. Who is Mr. Smedley? What does he prophesy about Chester?

Name________________________________

Chapters Six—Ten (Pages 43-95)

18. Why does Mario go to Chinatown?
19. Who is Sai Fong?
20. What is the story of the first cricket, as told by Sai Fong?
21. What does Mario purchase from Sai Fong, what does it look like, how much does it cost, and why does it have that price?
22. What is Mario's fortune on the piece of paper taken from the fortune cookie?
23. Why doesn't Tucker Mouse want to live in Chinatown?
24. How does Chester feel about staying in the cage?
25. How does Tucker change the inside of the cage for his use?
26. What happens while Chester is dreaming about eating a leaf in Connecticut?
27. How does Mama Bellini react when she discovers what has happened to the two dollar bill?
28. What is Chester's "sentence"?
29. How does Tucker help Chester?
30. Why do Mario and Chester go to see Sai Fong?
31. Where is Chester during the Chinese dinner?
32. Where do the Chinese men find the answer for Chester's problem? What is the answer?
33. Why are Chester, Tucker and Harry having a party? Which one provides the food and drink?
34. What do Chester, Tucker and Harry do to entertain one another?
35. What happens while Tucker dances?

Chapters Eleven—Fifteen (Pages 97-151)

36. What does Chester do after the newsstand fire? Why?
37. How does Mama Bellini react when she sees the newsstand after the fire?
38. What does Mama Bellini call Chester? What is "good luck going backwards"?
39. What happens to Mama Bellini when Chester starts to chirp?
40. Why does Chester Cricket need a manager?
41. How does Chester start to learn new songs?
42. What does Mr. Smedley think of Chester's talent?
43. How does Mr. Smedley share the news of Chester's talent?
44. What happens after Mr. Smedley's letter is published in the *Times*?
45. When does Chester give concerts?
46. How is the newsstand business affected by Chester's concerts?
47. How does Chester feel about the concerts?
48. How does the thought of September affect Chester?
49. Why does Chester decide to retire?
50. Why does Chester think he entertains with his music in Connecticut?
51. What do Harry, Chester and Tucker do on Thursday night?
52. What does Chester take with him as a memento?
53. How will Chester know that he is in Connecticut?
54. How does Mario know that Chester is gone for good?
55. What do Harry and Tucker think of doing the following summer?

Name________________________

Vocabulary

scrounging (1)	glimmering (6)	shriek (6)	babble (7)
refuse (10)	rummaged (12)	wheezed (13)	scornfully (16)
resigned (16)	eavesdropping (18)	wistfully (20)	sympathetically (24)
frantic (27)	refined (31)	instinct (40)	prophesy (41)

Make a special word map for ten of the above vocabulary words taken from Chapters One through Five. Before following the word map pattern given below, turn to the pages in the book on which the word appears. Look at how each word is used.

Synonyms
(words with the same meaning)

____
____
____
____

Magazine Cutout or Your Sketch to Show What the Word Means

Word

____

Definition in Your Own Words

____
____
____
____

Word Used in a Sentence

____
____
____
____

Name____________________________

RE + [ ] = REBUS

Vocabulary Words Used For This Activity:
secondhand (3) forepaws (27) neon (32) incense (46) browse (53)

Directions: Use the letters and the pictures to figure out the words.

1. [ ] + E = ________________

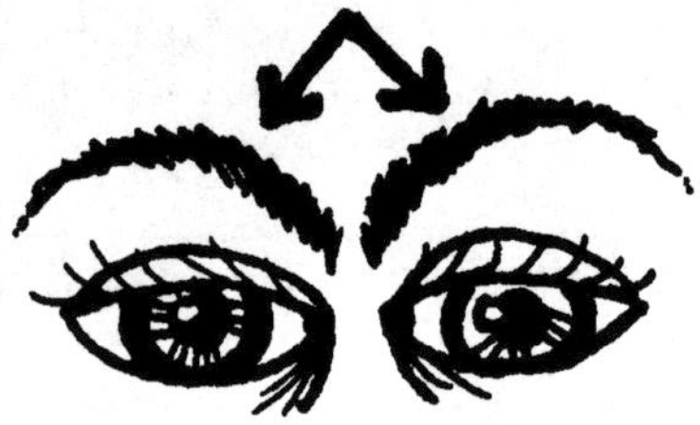

2. [- K - E] + [1 - E] = ________________

3. IN + [- T] + E = ________________

4. [4 - U] + E + [ ] = ________________

5. [FIRST] = ________________

Make your own REBUS

6.

7.

Name______________________________

Vocabulary—Synonym or Antonym?

subsided (2)	scooted (18)	forlornly (26)	cautiously (27)
frantic (27)	refined (31)	leery (31)	abrupt (43)
toppled (43)	cluttered (46)	emphasize (48)	admiration (53)

Directions: Match the synonym or antonym in the comparison with a listed vocabulary word.

Sample: BETTER is to WORSE as RIGHT is to WRONG.

1. NUISANCE is to BOTHER as ________________ is to SUDDEN.
2. SLOW is to FLEET as ________________ is to CONTEMPT.
3. PLEASANT is to CANTANKEROUS as ________________ is to ASCENDED.
4. UNOCCUPIED is to VACANT as ________________ is to DISORDERLY.
5. HUMBLE is to ARROGANT as ________________ is to RECKLESSLY.
6. CONFUSING is to PERPLEXING as ________________ is to ABATED.
7. PLEASE is to RILE as ________________ is to VULGAR.
8. ALIVE is to EXTINCT as ________________ is to COMPOSED.
9. INTERFERE is to MEDDLE as ________________ is to ACCENTUATE.
10. STAY is to LEAVE as ________________ is to CHEERFULLY.
11. DISLIKE is to ADMIRE as ________________ is to TRUSTFUL.
12. TOLERATE is to ENDURE as ________________ is to SCAMPERED.

Name______________________________

Vocabulary

lurched (43)	craned (44)	delightedly (45)	kimonos (46)
incense (46)	emphasize (48)	gaping (53)	pranced (54)
burrowed (60)	gust (61)	concentrated (64)	denounced (66)
bail (68)	heave (68)	resolved (69)	peril (70)

Directions: Write the vocabulary word that matches each definition or synonym.

1. ______________________________ joyfully, rapturously

2. ______________________________ tunneled, dug

3. ______________________________ decided, planned

4. ______________________________ focused, studied

5. ______________________________ staring, gazing

6. ______________________________ deposit, pledge

7. ______________________________ swaggered, strutted

8. ______________________________ sling, hoist, hurl

9. ______________________________ stress, accentuate

10. ______________________________ condemned, castigated

Name______________________________

Vocabulary Crossword Puzzle

Directions: Use the clues to figure out the answers to the crossword.

Name______________________________

Vocabulary Word Search

Directions: Do the word search. Find the words on the horizontal, vertical and diagonal. Write down the letters that have not been used, starting at the top and working left to right in each row. Group the letters into words to find the hidden message.

T	A	A	C	O	N	C	E	R	T	O	X	G	D	S
L	U	S	R	F	C	K	E	R	U	N	N	E	E	T
E	Y	C	T	S	L	S	E	S	I	I	T	R	I	C
X	R	R	O	H	O	E	H	J	Z	A	O	M	O	O
H	E	I	I	M	M	N	X	A	L	C	M	S	V	N
A	L	S	A	C	P	A	G	U	N	U	V	I	A	T
U	I	N	G	S	S	O	T	E	S	T	O	B	T	R
S	E	A	I	L	E	A	S	A	R	C	H	E	I	A
T	V	S	T	L	R	E	F	I	M	O	M	E	O	L
I	E	R	F	G	R	O	U	I	T	B	D	A	N	T
N	D	F	N	U	H	T	O	F	R	I	L	E	Z	O
G	U	O	T	C	H	I	S	C	A	E	O	I	N	E
M	C	S	R	H	O	R	I	Z	O	N	B	N	N	T
G	E	U	C	E	L	E	B	R	I	T	Y	U	S	G
G	L	C	O	M	P	A	R	T	M	E	N	T	G	E

AMBLING
ARSON
ASTHMA
CELEBRITY
COMPARTMENT
COMPOSITIONS
CONCERTO
CONGRATULATED
CONTRALTO
ENCORES
EXHAUSTING
FIREBUG
FLEX
GAZING
GESTURE
HORIZON
JINX
LURCH
LYRICS
MAZE
MUFFLE
OVATION
RELIEVED
RODENT
SUMMIT

HIDDEN MESSAGE:

____

Name______________________________

Vocabulary Acrostic

Vocabulary Words

scrounging (1)	secondhand (3)	shriek (6)	eavesdropping (18)
wistfully (20)	moaned (22)	sympathetically (24)	chirp (26)
expert (28)	leery (31)	dunked (36)	prophesy (41)

Directions: Find the missing word for each clue. Write the letters of the word in the space above the numbers. Then transfer the numbered letters to the numbered spaces at the end of the activity. An old saying that Chester might be thinking of will appear.

Definition Clue

1. predict, forecast — _ _ _ _ _ _ _ _ (20, 22)

2. used, old — _ _ _ _ _ _ _ _ _ _ (7, 13, 2)

3. wishfully, yearningly — _ _ _ _ _ _ _ _ _ (16, 1, 11, 15)

4. screech, scream — _ _ _ _ _ _ (18, 17)

5. groaned, lamented — _ _ _ _ _ _ (9, 14)

6. listening, overhearing — _ _ _ _ _ _ _ _ _ _ _ _ _ (3, 4, 10, 8)

7. compassionately — _ _ _ _ _ _ _ _ _ _ _ _ _ _ _ (21, 19, 5, 6, 12)

Name______________________________

Transfer numbered letters here. Make an illustration to go with the saying.

___ ___ ___ ___ ___   ___ ___   ___ ___
1 2 3 4 5   6 7   8 9

___ ___ ___ ___ ___   ___ ___ ___ ___
10 11 12 13 14   15 16 17 18

___ ___ ___ ___
19 20 21 22

Name______________________________

Vocabulary Review

smoldering (97)	monkeying (98)	downhearted (98)	asthma (98)
firebug (99)	solemnly (107)	rodent (108)	sublime (115)
throngs (123)	exhausting (124)	entomologist (128)	horizon (132)
gesture (134)	fascinated (138)	maze (147)	lurch (148)

Directions: Complete each statement with a word from the box above.

1. Mama Bellini suffers from _ _ _ _ _ _.
   29

2. Mama Bellini thinks Chester is a _ _ _ _ _ _ _.
   10 12

3. Tucker is a _ _ _ _ _ _.
   11 4 30 6

4. Chester finds his schedule _ _ _ _ _ _ _ _ _ _.
   9 23 26 32 22

5. Chester feels _ _ _ _ _ _ _ _ _ _ _ after the newsstand fire.
   15 16 13 5 7 18 31

6. _ _ _ _ _ _ _ of people came to hear Chester play.
   1 2

7. The train gave a _ _ _ _ _ forward after Chester got on it.
   8 27 28

Name________________________________

8. Chester dreamed of seeing smoke on the __ __ __ __ __ __ __ __ from burning leaves.
(19 21 25 14)

9. Tucker thinks seriously and __ __ __ __ __ __ __ __ about Chester's retirement.
(24)

10. Mr. Smedley thinks Chester's music is __ __ __ __ __ __ __ __.
(20 3 17)

Directions: Notice the numbers under some of the letters you have written. Place the correct letter with its matching number on each line below to read an African proverb that might be placed at the end of the story.

___ ___ ___ ___   ___   ___ ___ ___ ___
1 2 3 4   5   6 7 8 9

___ ___ ___ ___ ___ ___   ___ ___ ___ ___
10 11 12 13 14 15   16 17 18 19

___ ___ ___ ___   ___ ___ ___ ___
20 21 22 23   24 25 26 27

___ ___ ___ ___ ___
28 29 30 31 32

Name________________________________

Scrambled Words

Vocabulary Words

amateur (87)	melancholy (101)	sublime (115)	illustrious (116)
throngs (123)	ambling (131)	fascinated (138)	muffle (146)

Directions: Unscramble each word. Draw a line to the definition. Include the word in a sentence.

Scrambled Words	Unscrambled Words	Definitions
1. f e m l u f	____________________	a. grand, lofty
2. m l u e i s b	____________________	b. layman
3. b g a l n m i	____________________	c. tone down
4. g o h t s r n	____________________	d. unhappy, sad
5. t r a a e m u	____________________	e. spellbound
6. s i d f t a c n a e	____________________	f. famous
7. h c y m a l l o e n	____________________	g. strolling
8. u s t s l i r u i l o	____________________	h. crowds

Sentences:

1. ____
2. ____
3. ____
4. ____
5. ____
6. ____
7. ____
8. ____

Name______________________________

Synonyms

Directions: Add to the synonym trains begun below. After thinking of all you can on your own, use a dictionary and a thesaurus to find more synonyms. You may also add related words such as antonyms, but be sure to label them.

1. **honorable** - trustworthy -
2. **gilded** - embellished -
3. **fidget** - squirm -
4. **gamboling** - frolicking -
5. **peril** - danger -
6. **skinflint** - miser -
7. **deduction** - inference -
8. **admiration** - esteem -
9. **scorched** - seared -
10. **muffle** - tone down -

Name______________________________

Descriptions

Directions: Use each letter of Chester's name as the first letter of a descriptive word.

C harming
H______________________________
E______________________________
S______________________________
T______________________________
E______________________________
R______________________________

C______________________________
R______________________________
I______________________________
C______________________________
K______________________________
E______________________________
T______________________________

Directions: Write a paragraph in which you describe Chester Cricket or one of his adventures.

____
____
____
____
____

Name______________________________

Quatrain Poetry

A **quatrain** is a poem written in four lines. It may be rhymed or unrhymed. When the poem rhymes, it may have a variety of rhyming patterns. The author decides on the rhyme pattern.

Directions: Write a quatrain poem about one of the characters or situations in the story of *The Cricket in Times Square.* Make an illustration for your poem.

____

____

____

____

Name________________________________

Cryptogram

As Chester plays, the crowd at the station becomes silent. The author describes the phenomenon on page 138.

Directions: Decode the following to discover how the author describes the silence.

(For the following cryptogram, you will need to discover the code used to encrypt the quote. Use the hints given to determine the code, and then use the code to decipher the quote. Fill in the letter above the line that corresponds to the code representation below the line. Hints: "Z" represents the letter "A," "H" represents the letter "S," "K" represents the letter "P," and "D" represents the letter "W." Is there a pattern to the letters?)

____ ______ ______ _ ____ ______ ____
ORPV IRKKOVH ZILFMW Z HGLMV WILKKVW RMGL

_____ _____ ___ _______ __ _______ ______
HGROO DZGVI GSV XRIXOVH LU HROVMXV HKIVZW

___ ____ ___ _________
LFG UILN GSV MVDHHGZMW

Name_______________________________

Story Review Crossword Puzzle

Directions: Use the clues to figure out the answers to the crossword.

Across

6 The first name of the boy who tends the newsstand
7 Chester's home state
9 Kind of leaf Chester eats
15 The name of the cricket in the story
16 Tucker learns a lot by doing this
19 The name of the mouse in the story
20 Mario's last name
22 Kind of sausage Chester likes to eat
23 Number of cents Mario is charged for the cricket cage
24 The shape of the cricket cage

Down

1 Where Chester sleeps (2 words)
2 Place where Mario buys the cricket cage
3 What Sai Fong collects
4 Last name of music teacher
5 The name of the cat in the story
8 Subway station where story takes place (2 words)
10 The thing that is at the top of the cricket cage
11 What Chester listens to in order to learn new songs
12 What Sai Fong sells in his store
13 What Mario uses to eat his Chinese dinner
14 Kind of pipe Tucker calls home
17 How Tucker gets his provisions
18 Mario's conductor friend
21 Mario's counterman friend

Name________________________________

Written Directions

Directions: Mickey, the counterman, makes Chester a soda in a table spoon. (page 38) Create a special concoction for Chester. Write the directions for the preparation and the serving of Chester's Concoction.

Chester's Concoction

Ingredients:

Preparation:

Serving:

Illustration:

Name_______________________________

Creative Design

Directions: Mario purchases a cricket cage for Chester that is in the shape of a pagoda. (page 46) Design a cricket cage for Chester. Give the dimensions of the cage, the materials to be used to make it, and write instructions for its construction. Make an illustration of the cage.

Chester's Cricket Cage

Materials:

Dimensions:

Instructions:

Illustration:

Name______________________________

Fortune Cookie Sayings

Directions: Mr. Fong gives Mario his first fortune cookie. Inside the cookie is a piece of paper that tells Mario of good luck coming his way. (page 51) Make some good luck sayings on the lines below. Cut them apart and share them with others.

____

____

____

____

____

____

____

____

____

____

Name_______________________________

Tucker's Life Savings

Directions: Tucker has two dollars and ninety-three cents in coins. (page 70) The chart below shows the distribution of Tucker's coins. Fill in the chart with different combinations of coins that add up to a total of two dollars and ninety-three cents.

half dollars	quarters	dimes	nickels	pennies
2	5	2	6	18

Name______________________________

New York City Kriss Kross

Directions: This puzzle consists of a list of words and a blank puzzle structure. Solve the puzzle by placing the words into the puzzle.

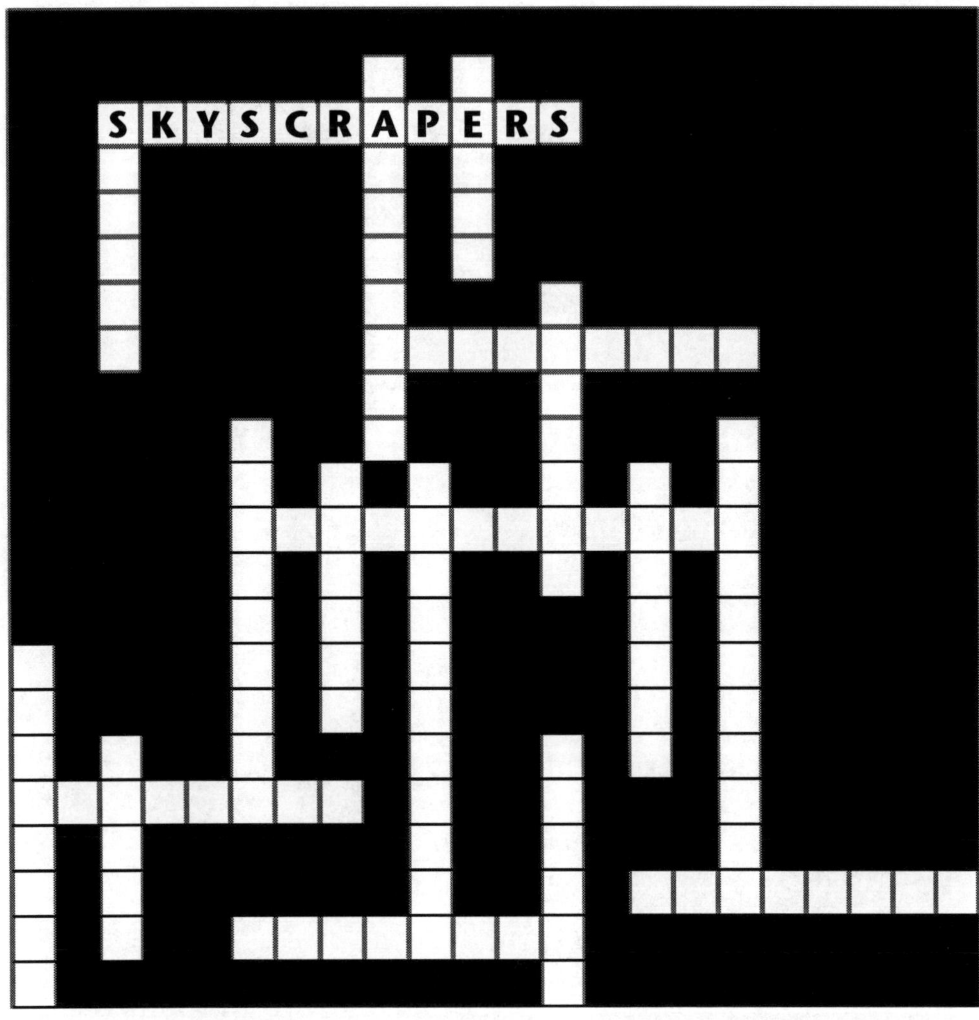

BRONX
FERRY
HARLEM
QUEENS
SUBWAY
DIVERSE
HARBORS
AIRPORTS
BOROUGHS
BROADWAY
BROOKLYN
EASTRIVER
MANHATTAN
TERMINALS
CENTRALPARK
HUDSONRIVER
SKYSCRAPERS
STATENISLAND

Name______________________________

The Cricket in Times Square
Comprehension Quiz
Correcting True-False
Chapters One—Ten, Pages 1-95

Directions: Label each statement "T" for True or "F" for False. Change the false statements into true ones by changing some of the words or by rewriting the statement.

______ 1. This story takes place in New York City.

______ 2. Tucker is a cat.

______ 3. Chester Cricket is from Connecticut.

______ 4. Mickey tends the newsstand for his father.

______ 5. The newsstand is in the subway station.

______ 6. Harry Cat and Tucker Mouse are friends.

______ 7. Harry and Tucker live in a drain pipe in the subway.

______ 8. Tucker is Mario's pet.

______ 9. Sai Fong sells Mario a cricket cage.

______ 10. The cricket cage is in the shape of the Leaning Tower.

______ 11. Tucker gives two dollars of his savings to help Chester.

______ 12. Sai Fong prepares an Italian dinner for Mario and Chester.

______ 13. Sai Fong discovers that Chester should eat mulberry leaves.

______ 14. Harry, Tucker and Chester have a party.

______ 15. Harry dances at the party.

Name______________________________

The Cricket in Times Square
Comprehension Quiz
Advanced Level

Directions: Answer each question in one complete sentence. (Events are in story sequence.)

1. Where does this story take place?
2. What is Tucker?
3. Chester Cricket is from what state?
4. Who tends the newsstand for Papa Bellini on Saturday night?
5. Where is the newsstand located in New York?
6. Where do Tucker and Harry live?
7. What kind of a pet does Mario have?
8. What does Mario buy for his pet?
9. What does Chester eat from the cash drawer in the newsstand?
10. What does Tucker do to help Chester gain his freedom from the cage?
11. What kind of leaves does Sai Fong have for Chester?
12. Why do Harry, Tucker and Chester have a party?
13. What does Tucker bring to the party?
14. What does Chester do to entertain Harry and Tucker?
15. What does Tucker's dancing cause?

Name______________________________

Identification: Find a character on the right who matches the description on the left. Write the letter of the character next to the matching number. Each character is to be used only once.

______ 1.	He has a shop in Chinatown.	a. Paul
______ 2.	He makes a special soda for Chester.	b. Mario
______ 3.	She hums Italian songs to Chester's music.	c. Chester
		d. Sai Fong
______ 4.	He buys a cricket cage for Chester.	
		e. Papa Bellini
______ 5.	When he speaks in a certain quiet tone, that's all there is to it.	
		f. Mr. Smedley
______ 6.	He shares his life savings with Chester.	
		g. Mickey
______ 7.	He lives in a drain pipe with Tucker.	
		h. Tucker
______ 8.	He is a conductor friend of Mario's.	
		i. Mama Bellini
______ 9.	He is a music teacher.	
		j. Harry Cat
______ 10.	He sleeps in a matchbox.	

Name______________________________

Identification: Find a character on the right who matches the quote on the left. Write the letter of the character next to the matching number. Each character is to be used only once.

______	1.	"You're up awfully late tonight." (page 4)	a. Tucker
______	2.	"I dreamed it was a leaf and I ate it." (page 62)	b. Mr. Smedley
______	3.	"He's a firebug!" (page 99)	c. Paul
______	4.	"You know stoly of first clicket?" (page 48)	d. Harry
______	5.	"Why don't you let him stand on the rim?" (page 36)	e. Mama Bellini
______	6.	"Supposing I give you the rest of my life's savings." (page 101)	f. Papa Bellini
______	7.	"It makes me want to purr to hear it." (page 30)	g. Mario
______	8.	"Oh now, now. Mario couldn't help it if nobody buys." (page 15)	h. Chester
______	9.	"My cricket took it and went home." (page 149)	i. Mickey
______	10.	"He has absolute pitch." (page 112)	j. Sai Fong

Name____________________________

Directions: Fill in each blank with the correct word or phrase.

The story takes place in a 1. ________________ station in the city of 2. __________ ____________. The station is located at 3. ____________________________. Mr. and Mrs. 4. ___________________ have a 5. ________________________ in the subway station. 6. ____________________, their son, tends the business on Saturday night. Mario finds 7. ________________ Cricket, and takes him to the newsstand. The cricket becomes Mario's 8. _________________. Chester meets 9. ___________________ Mouse and 10. _________________ Cat at the newsstand. The mouse and the cat are the best of 11. ____________________. They live in an abandoned 12. _________________ pipe in the subway station. Mario buys Chester a 13. _________________ cage from 14. _______________, who has a shop in 15. _________________________. The cricket cage is in the shape of a Chinese 16. _________________. Sai Fong gives Mario and Chester a little 17. ____________________ to hang at the top of the cage. While dreaming, Chester accidentally eats part of a 18. ______________ dollar bill from the cash drawer. 19. __________________ gives Chester some of his life's 20. _____________________ to pay for the mistake. Sai Fong discovers that the leaves from the 21. _________________ tree in his yard are good for Chester to eat. 22. ___________________ becomes Chester's 23. ___________________. Chester Cricket gives 24. ______________ at the newsstand and becomes a 25. _____________________.

Name______________________________

Written Response

Directions: Write about two of the following items. Circle the letters of the two items that you select.

A. What do you think the author means by saying the following about Papa Bellini? "And when Papa spoke in a certain quiet tone—that was all there was to it. Even Mama didn't dare disagree." (pages 16-17)

B. Chester asks the following of Tucker: "But what would I be doing here? I'm a country cricket." (page 25) How would you reply to Chester?

C. When Chester tells Tucker that he thinks cats and mice are enemies, Tucker tells Chester that may be so in the country. "But in New York we gave up those old habits long ago. Harry is my oldest friend." (page 28) Explain the "old habits" of cats and mice. Do you think it is possible for the change to take place? Why or why not?

D. After Chester provides bail for Chester and releases him from the cage, Chester tells Tucker and Harry, "There's nothing like freedom." (page 54) Explain Chester's remark. Do you think Chester is one to abuse his freedom? Why or why not?

E. When discussing Chester's talents, Tucker tells Harry, "...talent is something rare and beautiful and precious, and it must not be allowed to go to waste." (page 107) What is your opinion of this statement? Do you agree or disagree with Tucker? Why?

____

____

____

____

____

____

____

Name______________________________

Multiple Choice: To the left of each item number, write the number of the BEST response.

______ 1. The story takes place in what city?
(1) Chicago
(2) Detroit
(3) London
(4) New York

______ 2. What kind of an animal is Tucker?
(1) cat
(2) mouse
(3) cricket
(4) dog

______ 3. Where does Tucker live in the subway station?
(1) newsstand
(2) vending machine
(3) drug store
(4) abandoned drain pipe

______ 4. What animal lives with Tucker?
(1) cat
(2) dog
(3) cricket
(4) mouse

______ 5. What kind of insect does Mario have for a pet?
(1) grasshopper
(2) cockroach
(3) cricket
(4) beetle

______ 6. What kind of business does the Bellini family have in the station?
(1) ice cream stand
(2) soft drink concession
(3) newsstand
(4) shoe shine store

Name______________________________

______ 7. What is the name of the cricket?
(1) Sam
(2) Chester
(3) Harry
(4) Toots

______ 8. What is the name of the cat?
(1) Sam
(2) Chester
(3) Harry
(4) Tucker

______ 9. Where is Sai Fong's shop located?
(1) Times Square
(2) Garden City
(3) Rockefeller Center
(4) Chinatown

______ 10. What does Mario purchase from Sai Fong?
(1) cricket cage
(2) umbrella
(3) kimono
(4) tea set

______ 11. What does Sai Fong give to Mario and Chester for the cage?
(1) pillow
(2) bed
(3) swing
(4) bell

______ 12. What is Mario's fortune from his cookie?
(1) good luck
(2) money
(3) pleasant dreams
(4) bad luck

______ 13. What does Tucker put in the cricket cage to sleep upon?
(1) blanket
(2) crisp dollar bill
(3) newspaper
(4) hay

Name________________________________

______14. What does Chester accidentally eat from the Bellini's cash register?
(1) part of a one dollar bill
(2) part of a five dollar bill
(3) part of a two dollar bill
(4) part of a ten dollar bill

______15. What kind of leaves does Sai Fong have for Chester?
(1) ginkgo
(2) maple
(3) mulberry
(4) oak

______16. What does Tucker's dancing cause at the anniversary party?
(1) fire
(2) flood
(3) avalanche
(4) rain

______17. What does Mama Bellini do when she hears Chester play?
(1) She kills the cricket.
(2) She throws the cricket out of the newsstand.
(3) She locks the cricket in the cage.
(4) She hums and sings along.

______18. How does Chester learn new music?
(1) Mr. Smedley gives him lessons.
(2) He listens to the radio.
(3) He listens to television.
(4) He listens to Mama Bellini.

______19. How does Chester share his talent and also help the Bellinis?
(1) He writes music and sells it.
(2) He gives Mr. Smedley lessons.
(3) He gives concerts at the newsstand.
(4) He appears on television.

______20. When Chester goes home, where does he go?
(1) Connecticut
(2) Chicago
(3) New Hampshire
(4) New Jersey

Answer Key

Answers—Study Questions

Chapters One—Five (Pages 1-41)

1. Tucker is a mouse. 2. Tucker lives in a drain pipe in the Times Square subway station. 3. Tucker scrounges for his food in the subway station. 4. Mario is a boy who tends his father's newsstand in the subway station every Saturday night. 5. A cricket causes the unusual sound heard by Mario and Tucker. 6. Mario takes the cricket to the newsstand. Mario makes a bed for the cricket out of a matchbox lined with a facial tissue. 7. Mama Bellini does not like bugs. She wants Mario to get rid of the cricket. Papa Bellini is more sympathetic to Mario. 8. Papa decides that Mario can keep the pet cricket at the newsstand. Mama reluctantly agrees. 9. Tucker's favorite activities are scrounging and eavesdropping on human beings. 10. Liverwurst is the cause of Chester's move from Connecticut to New York. 11. Chester is transported in a picnic basket from Connecticut to New York. He is stuck under roast beef sandwiches and cannot get out. 12. Tucker explains to Chester that in New York cats and mice are not enemies. "We gave up those old habits long ago." Harry is Tucker's best friend. 13. Tucker and Harry think that the future of the newsstand is not good. "They're going broke fast." 14. A long-hair is "an extra refined person," according to Tucker. 15. That night, Chester looks up and sees "a star that he knew was a star he used to look at back in Connecticut." 16. Chester's food back in the meadow consists of leaves and grass, and sometimes a piece of tender bark. 17. Mr. Smedley is the Bellini's best customer. He is a music teacher. Mr. Smedley predicts the Chester might play as well as Orpheus. "I prophesy great things for a creature of such ability."

Chapters Six—Ten (Pages 43-95)

18. Mario wants to buy a cricket cage for Chester in Chinatown. 19. Sai Fong is the proprietor of a store in Chinatown. 20. The story is about a man, Hsi Shuai, who speaks only the truth. Wicked men, who are unhappy hearing the truth, decide to kill Hsi Shuai. High gods change Hsi Shuai into a cricket. The song of the cricket is the "song of one who still speaks tluth and knows all things." 21. Mario purchases a pagoda cricket cage for fifteen cents from Sai Fong. Sai Fong charges that amount "because this clicket so lemarkable." 22. Mario's fortune in the cookie is, "GOOD LUCK IS COMING YOUR WAY." 23. Tucker knows that there are such foods as bird's nests soup and sharks' fins stew. He is afraid that he might be made into a soufflé. 24. Chester doesn't want to stay in the cage. It makes him nervous. He thinks that there is "nothing like freedom." 25. Tucker uses dollar bills, one as a sheet under him and one as a cover. He also uses an earring as a pillow. 26. Chester is actually eating part of a two dollar bill while he dreams about eating a leaf. 27. Mama Bellini is angry.

She throws a magazine at Tucker, tosses Chester into his cage and knits furiously. 28. Chester has to stay in the cage until Mario can replace the money. 29. Tucker decides to donate most of his savings to Chester so the money can be repaid. 30. Mario decides that something is wrong with Chester's diet and seeks the of advice of Mr. Fong in Chinatown. 31. Chester is in his cage. The cage is placed in the center of the dining table. 32. The men find the answer for Chester's problem in a big book. Mario needs to feed Chester mulberry leaves. Mr. Fong has a mulberry tree in his yard. 33. The three friends are having a party to celebrate the fact that it has been exactly two months since his arrival in New York. Tucker provides the food and drink. 34. Harry sings, Tucker dances, and Chester plays songs with his wings. 35. While Tucker dances, he accidentally knocks some kitchen matches onto the cement floor. A fire starts. Chester sets off the alarm clock to attract attention.

Chapters Eleven—Fifteen (Pages 97-151)

36. Chester returns to the newsstand. He doesn't want the Bellinis to think that he started the fire. 37. Mama moans, wheezes from asthma, and sobs. 38. Mama calls Chester a firebug and a jinx—"good luck going backwards." 39. When Mama hears Chester's songs, she sings and hums along. The songs remind Mama of good times in the past. She decides that any cricket that can chirp like Chester wouldn't start a fire. 40. Chester needs a manager so his talents do not go to waste, and so the Bellinis and Tucker will become financially secure. 41. Chester learns new songs by listening to the radio. 42. Mr. Smedley thinks Chester is a musical miracle. 43. Mr. Smedley shares the news of Chester's talent by writing a letter to the musical editor of the *New York Times*. 44. After the letter is published in the newspaper, Chester becomes a celebrity. Large crowds come to hear Chester play. 45. Chester's concerts are at eight o'clock in the morning and at four-thirty in the afternoon, when there is a large crowd of people in the station. 46. The newsstand business booms. 47. Chester's concert schedule makes him tired. He misses the fun and freedom of the time before the concerts. Chester is not happy. 48. The thought of September makes Chester feel small and lost. 49. Chester decides to retire because he misses his home in Connecticut. 50. Chester entertains "woodchucks and pheasants and ducks and rabbits, and everybody else who lives in the meadow or the brook." 51. Harry, Chester and Tucker have a party in Tucker's drain pipe in honor of Chester's retirement. 52. Chester takes the silver bell. 53. Chester tells Harry and Tucker, "I'll smell the trees and I'll feel the air, and I'll know." 54. Mario knows that Chester will not be back because the bell is gone. 55. Harry and Tucker think of making a trip to Connecticut the following summer.

Answers

Activity #1

1. T
2. F
3. T
4. T
5. F

Activity #2—Student Generated

Activity #3

1. browse
2. neon
3. incense
4. forepaws
5. secondhand

Activity #4

1. ABRUPT
2. ADMIRATION
3. TOPPLED
4. CLUTTERED
5. CAUTIOUSLY
6. SUBSIDED
7. REFINED
8. FRANTIC
9. EMPHASIZE
10. FORLORNLY
11. LEERY
12. SCOOTED

Activity #5

1. delightedly
2. burrowed
3. resolved
4. concentrated
5. gaping
6. bail
7. pranced
8. heave
9. emphasize
10. denounced

Activity #6: Vocabulary Crossword Puzzle—See page 43 of this guide.

Activity #7: Vocabulary Word Search—See page 43 of this guide.

Activity #8

1. P R O P H E S Y
   20 22

2. S E C O N D H A N D
   7 13 2

3. W I S T F U L L Y
16 1 11 15

4. S H R I E K
18 17

5. M O A N E D
9 14

6. E A V E S D R O P P I N G
3 4 10 8

7. S Y M P A T H E T I C A L L Y
21 19 5 6 12

T H E R E I S N O P L A C E L I K E H O M E
1 2 3 4 5 6 7 8 9 10 11 12 13 14 15 16 17 18 19 20 21 22

Activity #9

1. A S T H M A
29

2. F I R E B U G
10 12

3. R O D E N T
11 4 30 6

4. E X H A U S T I N G
9 23 26 32 22

5. D O W N H E A R T E D
15 16 13 5 7 18 31

6. T H R O N G S
1 2

7. L U R C H
8 27 28

8. H O R I Z O N
19 21 25 14

9. S O L E M N L Y
24

10. S U B L I M E
20 3 17

H O L D A T R U E F R I E N D W I T H B O T H Y O U R
1 2 3 4 5 6 7 8 9 10 11 12 13 14 15 16 17 18 19 20 21 22 23 24 25 26 27

H A N D S
28 29 30 31 32

Activity #10: Scrambled Words

1. muffle - c (tone down)
2. sublime - a (grand, lofty)

3. ambling - g (strolling)
4. throngs - h (crowds)
5. amateur - b (layman)
6. fascinated - e (spellbound)
7. melancholy - d (unhappy, sad)
8. illustrious - f (famous)

Activity #11: Synonym Trains, Answers will vary—Student generated

Activity #12: Written Descriptions, Answers will vary—Student generated

Activity #13: Original poem

Activity #14: Cryptogram—See page 44 of this guide.

Activity #15: Story Review Crossword Puzzle—See page 44 of this guide.

Activities 16, 17 & 18—Student generated

Activity #19—examples follow:

50	25	10	05	01
2	5	2	6	18
4	3	1	1	3
4	2	4	0	3
4	1	6	1	3
4	0	9	0	3
4	0	8	2	3
4	0	7	4	3
4	0	6	6	3
4	0	5	8	3
4	0	4	10	3

Activity #20: New York City Kriss Kross—See page 44 of this guide.

Comprehension Quiz (Chapters One—Ten)

1 - T
2 - F (MOUSE)
3 - T
4 - F (MARIO)
5 - T
6 - T
7 - T
8 - F (CHESTER)
9 - T
10 - F (PAGODA)
11 - T
12 - F (CHINESE)
13 - T
14 - T
15 - F (TUCKER)

Comprehension Quiz—Advanced Level

1. The story takes place in the Times Square subway station in the city of New York.
2. Tucker is a mouse.
3. Chester Cricket is from the state of Connecticut.
4. Mario tends the newsstand for his father on Saturday night.
5. The newsstand is located in the Times Square subway station.
6. Tucker and Harry live in a drain pipe in the station.
7. Chester Cricket is Mario's pet.
8. Mario buys a cricket cage for Chester.
9. Chester eats part of a two dollar bill from the cash drawer.
10. Tucker gives Chester two dollars of his savings.
11. Sai Fong has mulberry leaves for Chester.
12. Harry, Tucker, and Chester have a party to celebrate Chester's two months in New York.
13. Tucker brings the refreshments to the party.
14. Chester plays for his friends.
15. Tucker's dancing causes a fire at the newsstand.

Novel Test: Identification

1. - d (Sai Fong)
2. - g (Mickey)
3. - i (Mama Bellini)
4. - b (Mario)
5. - e (Papa Bellini)
6. - h (Tucker)
7. - j (Harry Cat)
8. - a (Paul)
9. - f (Mr. Smedley)
10. - c (Chester)

Novel Test: Identification—Advanced Level

1. - c (Paul)
2. - h (Chester)
3. - e (Mama Bellini)
4. - j (Sai Fong)
5. - i (Mickey)
6. - a (Tucker)
7. - d (Harry)
8. - f (Papa Bellini)
9. - g (Mario)
10. - b (Mr. Smedley)

Novel Test: Fill-ins

1. subway
2. New York
3. Times Square
4. Bellini
5. newsstand
6. Mario
7. Chester
8. pet
9. Tucker
10. Harry
11. friends
12. drain
13. cricket
14. Sai Fong
15. Chinatown
16. pagoda
17. bell
18. two
19. Tucker
20. savings
21. mulberry
22. Tucker
23. manager
24. concerts
25. celebrity

Novel Test: Multiple Choice

1. - 4 (New York)
2. - 2 (mouse)
3. - 4 (abandoned drain pipe)
4. - 1 (cat)
5. - 3 (cricket)
6. - 3 (newsstand)
7. - 2 (Chester)
8. - 3 (Harry)
9. - 4 (Chinatown)
10. - 1 (cricket cage)
11. - 4 (bell)
12. - 1 (good luck)
13. - 2 (crisp dollar bill)
14. - 3 (part of a two dollar bill)
15. - 3 (mulberry)
16. - 1 (fire)
17. - 4 (She hums and sings along.)
18. - 2 (He listens to the radio.)
19. - 3 (He gives concerts at the newsstand.)
20. - 1 (Connecticut)

Activity #6: Vocabulary Crossword Puzzle

Activity #7: Vocabulary Word Search

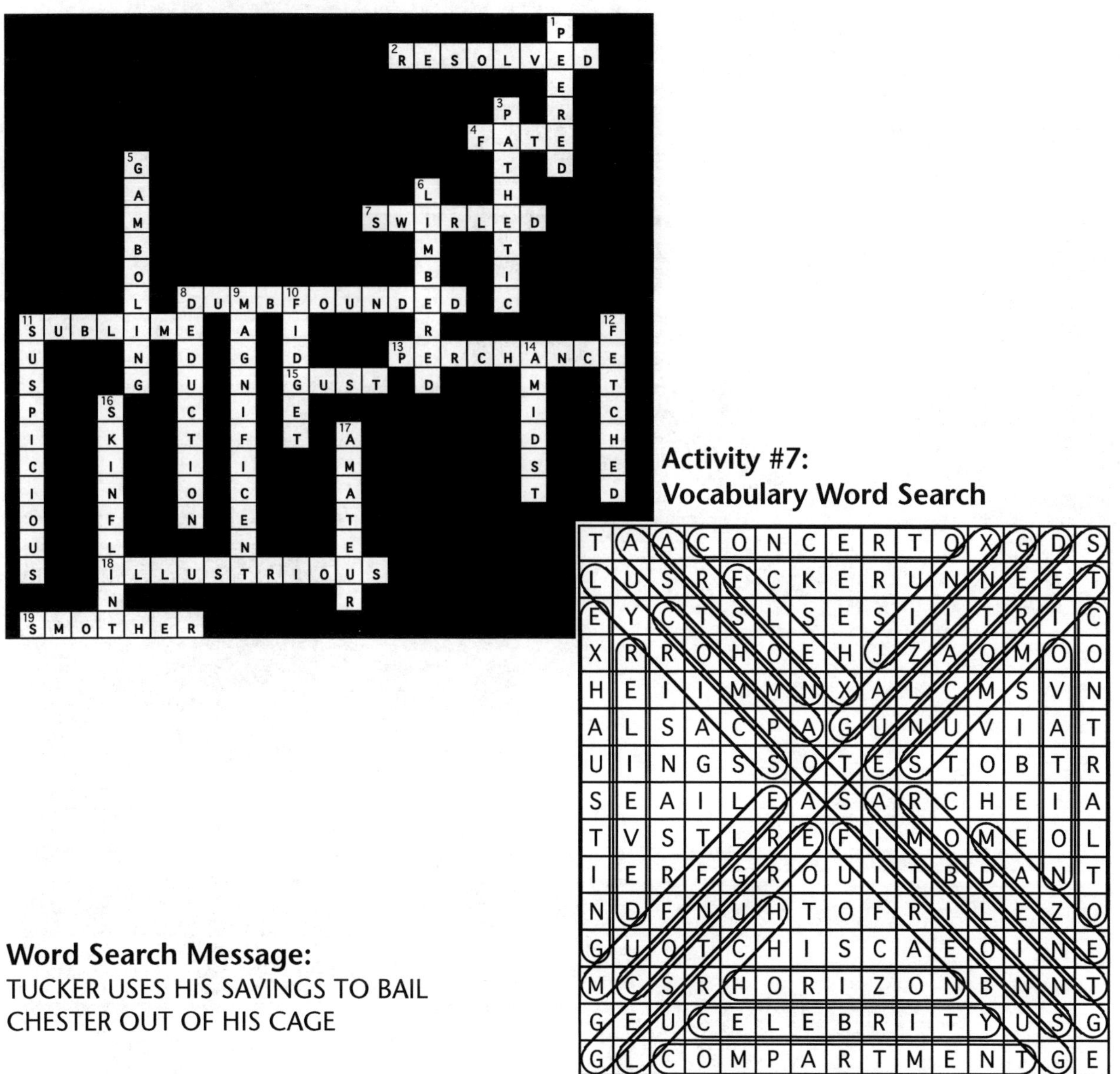

Word Search Message:
TUCKER USES HIS SAVINGS TO BAIL CHESTER OUT OF HIS CAGE

Activity #14: Cryptogram

(Note: The pattern of letters is the alphabet backwards.)

LIKE	RIPPLES	AROUND	A	STONE	DROPPED	INTO
ORPV	IRKKOVH	ZILFMW	Z	HGLMV	WILKKVW	RMGL

STILL	WATER	THE	CIRCLES	OF	SILENCE	SPREAD
HGROO	DZGVI	GSV	XRIXOVH	LU	HROVMXV	HKIVZW

OUT	FROM	THE	NEWSSTAND
LFG	UILN	GSV	MVDHHGZMW

Activity #15: Story Review Crossword Puzzle

Activity #20: New York City Kriss Kross

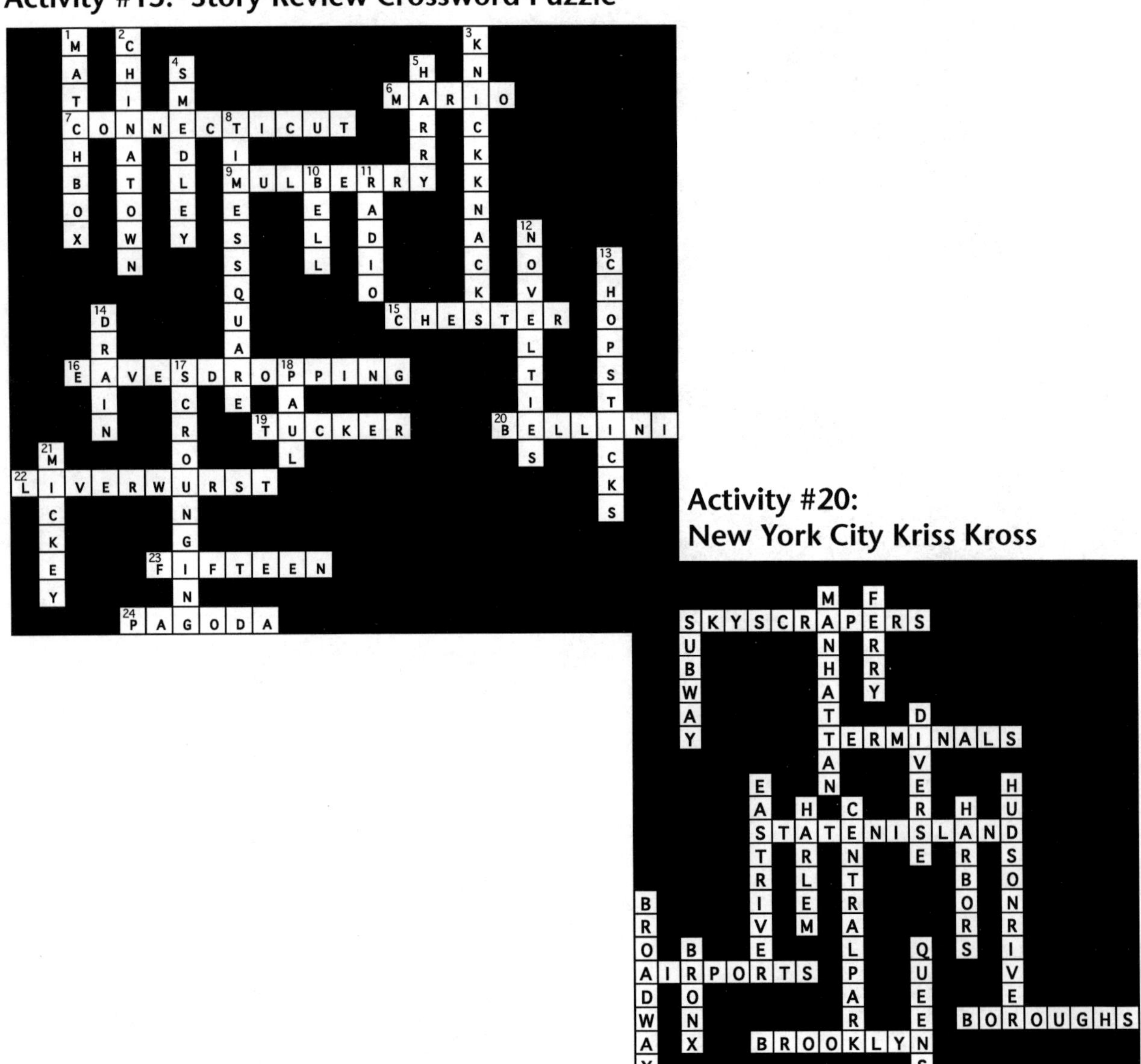